DECLARATION

•

I hereby declare that
all the paper produced
by Cartiere del Garda S.p.A.
in its Riva del Garda mill
is manufactured completely
Acid-free and Wood-free

Dr. Alois Lueftinger
Managing Director and General Manager
Cartiere del Garda S.p.A.

G R E E N   W O R L D

FIR TREES

Written by
Theresa Greenaway

STECK-VAUGHN
L I B R A R Y
A Division of Steck-Vaughn Company

Austin, Texas

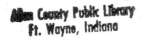
**Published in the United States in 1990
by Steck-Vaughn, Co., Austin, Texas,**
a subsidiary of National Education Corporation

A Templar Book
Devised and produced by The Templar Company plc
Pippbrook Mill, London Road, Dorking, Surrey RH4 1JE, Great Britain
Copyright © 1990 by The Templar Company plc

Editor: Wendy Madgwick
Designer: Jane Hunt
Illustrators: David Moore, John Rignall and Brian Watson

Notes to Reader
There are some words in this book that are printed in **bold** type.
A brief explanation of these words is given in the glossary on p. 44.

All living things are given two Latin names when first classified by a
scientist. Some of them also have a common name, for example
noble fir, *Abies nobilis.* In this book, the common name is used where
possible, but the scientific name is given when first mentioned.

Library of Congress Cataloging-in-Publication Data
Greenaway, Theresa, 1947–
Fir trees. (The Green World) "A Templar Book" – T.p. verso.
Includes bibliographical references.
Summary: Introduces the conifer and fir trees of the world and discusses
products we get from them, acid rain, forest wildlife, and the timber industry.
ISBN 0-8114-2727-7
1. Conifers – Juvenile literature. 2. Forests and forestry – Juvenile literature.
[1. Conifers. 2. Forests and forestry.]
I. Title. II. Series.
QK494.G74 1990 90-9640
585'.2 CIP AC

Color separations by Positive Colour Ltd, Maldon, Essex, Great Britain
Printed and bound by L.E.G.O., Vicenza, Italy
1 2 3 4 5 6 7 8 9 0 LE 94 93 92 91 90

Photographic credits
t = top, b = bottom, l = left, r = right
Cover: Bruce Coleman; page 10 Frank Lane/Eric & David Hosking;
page 11 Bruce Coleman/L.C. Marigo; page 13 Frank Lane/M. Nimmo;
page 14 Bruce Coleman/M.T. O'Keefe; page 17l Bruce Coleman/
G. Cubitt; page 18t New Zealand Forest Pulp and Paper; page 18b Bruce
Coleman, G.G. Hunter; page 20 Frank Lane/Silvestris; page 22 Frank
Lane/L. West; page 24 Bruce Coleman/Hans Reinhard; page 29 Bruce
Coleman/P. Helo; page 30 Frank Lane/M. Nimmo; page 37 Bruce
Coleman/Hans Reinhard; page 39t Bruce Coleman/G. Dore;
page 39b Bruce Coleman/S. Kaufman; page 41 Bruce Coleman/
F. Lanting; page 42 Bruce Coleman.

CONTENTS

Green World.. 6

Conifers or Fir Trees 8

Conifers of the World....................... 10

Conifers of Europe 12

North American Firs 14

Conifers of Asia 16

Conifers of the South 18

Trunks and Roots............................. 20

Leaves 22

Making Seeds 24

Seed Dispersal................................. 26

Conifers of the Cold 28

Mild, Moist Forests......................... 30

Human-Made Forests....................... 32

The Living Forest............................. 34

Acid Rain... 36

The Timber Industry 38

Paper-Making 40

Uses Past and Present 42

Glossary 44

Conifers in This Book 45

Further Reading............................... 45

Index.. 46

GREEN WORLD

This tree shows the different groups of plants that are found in the world. It does not show how they developed or their relationship with each other.

GINKGO

CYCADS

GNETATAE

FLOWERING PLANTS (Angiosperms)

NAKED SEEDED PLANTS (Gymnosperms)

CONIFERS

FERNS

MOSSES

FUNGI AND LICHENS

ALGAE

- Narrow needle-leaved trees or bushes
- Seeds develop in woody cones or fleshy cups
- About 520 species in seven families

Group 1
Monkey puzzle family (Araucariaceae)
- Often broad needles
- The cones have one-seeded scales

Group 2
Pine family (Pinaceae)
- Needles are arranged spirally
- Cones have two-seeded scales

Group 3
Redwood family (Taxodiaceae)
- Mostly have spirally arranged needles
- Cones often have more than two seeds on each scale

Group 4
Cypress family (Cupressaceae)
- Leaves are usually scalelike, sometimes short needles
- They are opposite or in whorls of three
- Most cones are small, round, and woody, but junipers have fleshy cones

Group 5
Yellow-wood family (Podocarpaceae)
- No cones – the scale is fleshy and covers the seed

Group 6
Plum yew family (Cephalotaxaceae)
- No cones – each seed is completely enclosed by the fleshy scale

Group 7
Yew family (Taxaceae)
- Needles are spirally arranged
- Each seed sits in a fleshy cup

The land area of the world is divided into ten main zones depending on the plants that grow there. Conifers are mostly found in the northern hemisphere; few grow in the southern hemisphere.

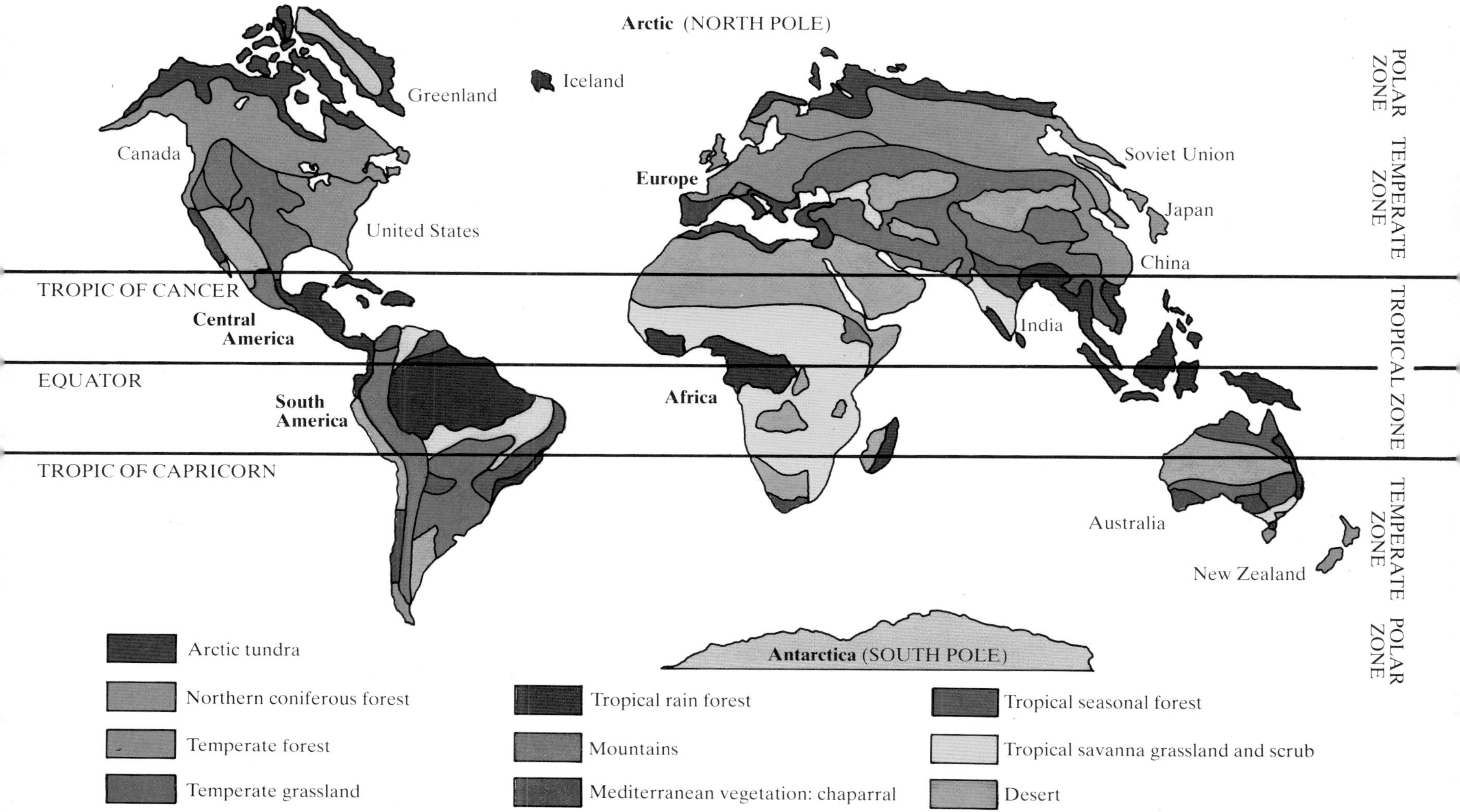

POLAR ZONE   TEMPERATE ZONE   TROPICAL ZONE   TEMPERATE ZONE   POLAR ZONE

Arctic (NORTH POLE)

Soviet Union
Japan
China
India
Iceland
Greenland
United States
Europe
Canada
Central America
South America
Africa
Australia
New Zealand
Antarctica (SOUTH POLE)

TROPIC OF CANCER
EQUATOR
TROPIC OF CAPRICORN

Arctic tundra
Northern coniferous forest
Temperate forest
Temperate grassland

Tropical rain forest
Mountains
Mediterranean vegetation: chaparral

Tropical seasonal forest
Tropical savanna grassland and scrub
Desert

CONIFERS OR FIR TREES

The conifers belong to a group of trees called **gymnosperms**. They differ from broad-leaved woodland trees because they have **cones** instead of flowers. Like flowers, the male cone produces the male sex cell, protected in a **pollen grain**, and the female cone produces the female sex cell or **ovule**. When these two cells fuse or join, a **seed** is formed (see p. 24). This seed will later develop into a new tree.

Most conifers are tall trees with narrow, spire-shaped branched tops called **crowns**, and long, straight, woody stems called trunks. A few are low bushes. If a tree seed sprouts in an unfavorable place, perhaps a dry, rocky crevice, it may never reach its full height.

Reach for the sky
Some of the world's tallest trees are conifers.

The tallest living tree is a coast redwood, the Howard Libbey tree. It is more than 360 feet high. (The second tallest is a broad-leaved tree, the Australian mountain ash.)

The third tallest is a noble fir (*Abies nobilis*), about 280 feet.

The tallest tree ever felled and measured was a Douglas fir (*Pseudotsuga menziesii*), which was 383 feet high.

North or South?

When the continents first formed, the climate was different in the northern and southern hemispheres. The early monkey puzzle trees became extinct in the northern part and now they only grow naturally in the southern hemisphere. The yellow-wood family is the largest group of conifers in the southern hemisphere. They are found in southern countries from Central and South America across to southern Asia and New Zealand.

Most early redwoods died out in the southern hemisphere; except for three species on the island of Tasmania, they only grow naturally in the north. The largest and most commercially important family of the northern hemisphere is the Pinaceae – pines, spruces, firs, and larches.

monkey puzzle
(*Araucaria araucana*)

sitka spruce
(*Picea sitchensis*)

The largest, and fourth tallest, tree is a giant sequoia the General Sherman tree. It is 272 feet tall, just over 78 feet round, and is estimated to weigh 2,230 tons!

- ■ Conifers are gymnosperms or cone-bearing trees.
- ■ The leaves are usually narrow and needle-shaped.
- ■ They are made up of roots, a thick, woody stem and a crown of branches and leaves.
- ■ There are about 520 species.

CONIFERS OF THE WORLD

The taiga is the world's largest band of coniferous forest. It stretches from Alaska, across northern Canada, northern Europe, and across the Soviet Union to its eastern shores, and covers 13 percent of the world's surface (see the map on p. 7). These forests are vast and the trees grow so close together that even walking through them is difficult. Huge areas, called **stands**, in which only one kind of conifer grows may stretch for many miles. The forests of Siberia are especially wild and remote.

The climate of the taiga is cool. Near the sea, plenty of rain may fall, but farther inland it is drier. The winters are long and dark, and the temperature is below 43°F for up to nine months of the year. Snows fall and the ground may freeze. During the short summer, the temperature only rises to about 50°F, but because of its northerly position, the summer days have long hours of daylight.

Siberia has the most extreme climate. Its winters are very severe with temperatures as low as –40°F. In contrast, its short summer is hot, with temperatures rising to over 104°F.

The northern forest
The taiga forests grow beyond the Arctic circle. At the northernmost limits, trees grow very slowly. Even trees over 70 years old have trunks no thicker than walking sticks.

Conifer forests of the southern hemisphere

The southern hemisphere has no equivalent to the taiga conifer forests. For one thing, there is less land in the south, especially in the temperate zone (see the map on p. 7). Southerly forests are often made up of conifer and broad-leaved trees. Many of the conifers are tall, long-lived trees, but they do not grow well outside their own regions, and so are not well known in the north.

Moist conifer forests of Northwest America

Along the west coast of North America, there is a strip of rich conifer forest. To the east rise the Coast Mountains, the Cascade Range, and the hills of the Sierra Nevada. These coastal forests are swept by rain, mists, and moist air rolling in from the Pacific Ocean. The climate is mild, and the conditions are ideal for conifer trees to grow. So it is not too surprising that most of the world's tallest trees are found there. The trunks grow straight and tall, and large numbers of the finest giants have been felled. However, some parts of these forests are now national parks or reserves. At the southern end of these forests, the climate is warmer and drier.

nooka cypress
(*Chamaecyparis nootkatensis*)

giant or grand fir
(*Abies grandis*)

CONIFERS OF EUROPE

Oak forests once covered the regions around the Mediterranean Sea, but these have mostly disappeared. Stone Age Neolithic people were the first to start clearing the trees, and the land has been farmed and grazed by sheep and goats ever since. Today, there are scattered pine forests throughout the region. On the Atlas Mountains of North Africa, the Corsican pine (*Pinus nigra*), and the Atlas cedar (*Cedrus atlantica*) flourish. Elsewhere, pines have invaded places once covered by oaks.

There are only three conifers native to the U.K.: the Scotch pine (*Pinus sylvestris*), the common juniper (*Juniperus communis*), and the yew (*Taxus baccata*). All three are also common elsewhere in Europe. Yew forests were once widespread on chalk downs. Most of this has now been cleared for farming. Yew is also poisonous to domestic animals.

**Scotch Pine
(*Pinus sylvestris*)**
Preferring dry, sandy soil, this tree can grow up to 115 feet. The upper trunk has reddish bark. The needles grow in pairs, and the cones are 1 – 2.3 inches long.

**European Silver Fir
(*Abies alba*)**
Up to 145 feet tall, this fir is a good timber tree. It grows on the slopes of central European mountains, up to 6,000 feet. The upright cones are about 4.7 inches long.

**Cedar of Lebanon
(*Cedrus libani*)**
A stately tree, growing up to 115 feet. The branches are fairly flat and grow out sideways, and the leaves are arranged in "tiers." The smooth, oblong cones are 6 inches long.

Stone pines

Maritime pine (*Pinus pinaster*) grows in France, Spain, and Portugal. The aleppo pine (*P. halepensis*) grows mostly in the eastern Mediterranean. The stone pine (*P. pinea*) can be recognized by its "umbrella" shaped crown.

Norway Spruce
(*Picea abies*)
This is a widely cultivated tree native to northern Europe. It grows up to 115 feet. The short needles are hard and pointed and the long cones (5 – 6 inches) hang down from the branch tips.

Corsican Pine
(*Pinus nigra* var. *maritima*)
From North Africa, Italy, and Corsica, this pine is planted in other parts of Europe for its good-quality wood. It grows up to 145 feet. The bark is dark gray, and the cones are about 2.3 inches long.

European Larch
(*Larix decidua*)
The larch is **deciduous** and sheds its leaves in autumn. Rosettes of pale green needles reappear in spring. The tree grows up to 145 feet high and has drooping twigs and thin-scaled cones 1.2 inches long.

13

NORTH AMERICAN FIRS

North America has provided the world with many of its finest timber-producing trees. A number of these are now grown commercially in other countries, for example the U.K. and most of Europe, Africa, Australia, and New Zealand, where they grow fast and well. People have also planted firs, spruces, pines, and cypresses as ornamental trees because of their pleasing appearance.

Swamp cypresses of the Everglades

The Everglades is an enormous freshwater swamp in the southernmost tip of Florida. It is about 13,000 square miles in area, and famous for its wildlife. Swamp cypresses are an important part of its vegetation. They are tall, graceful trees with green, leafy twigs that look like feathers. They can grow up to 125 to 150 feet tall. The unusual thing about them is that they can grow in shallow water as well as on dry land. Most trees cannot live in waterlogged soil because it does not contain enough oxygen. However, the roots of the swamp cypress grow projections, like bony knees, that stick up out of the water. These absorb all the oxygen the tree needs from the air. They are one of the few deciduous conifers and the leaves turn a bright reddish-brown in the autumn.

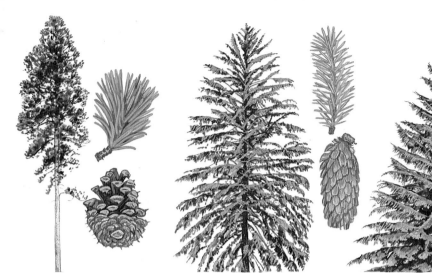

Lodgepole Pine
(*Pinus contorta*)

These were used by Native Americans as poles for their teepees. They grow to 85 feet in height, and their paired needles are twisted in shape. The cones are 2 inches long and each scale has a small, prickly spike.

Sitka Spruce
(*Picea sitchensis*)

A fast-growing tree, reaching about 160 feet, this spruce is planted for timber in moist, temperate regions worldwide. The needles are pointed and the 3-inch long cones have wavy-edged scales.

Western Hemlock
(*Tsuga heterophylla*)

This graceful tree with drooping branches can grow up to 250 feet in height. The needles are flat, blunt, and unequal in length, and the small, oval cones are less than an inch long.

Douglas Fir
(*Pseudotsuga menziesii*)

These 300-feet tall trees, which grow naturally in damp, ferny forests, are also planted elsewhere for ornament and timber. The needles are dark green and the cones are 2.7 inches long.

Coast Redwood
(*Sequoia sempervirens*)

The tallest tree in the world comes from California. The soft, fibrous bark is 120 inches thick, to protect it from forest fires. These giant trees have tiny cones, only about .7 inches long.

Western Red Cedar
(*Thuja plicata*)

The timber from this 130- to 200-foot tall tree is very resistant to decay. The leaves form glossy "scales," which cling closely to the twigs and have a fruity smell. The cones are tiny, only .5 inches long.

CONIFERS OF ASIA

The Himalayan mountains have the highest peaks in the world, including Mount Everest (29,028 feet). To the north lies Tibet, which is a high, almost treeless, flat plain or plateau. On the southern slopes, the forests contain a variety of trees. Many of these trees have commercial value and are also very important to the local people.

The villagers use the wood as fuel to cook and keep warm. In the 1970s, far too much of the forest was cut down. This resulted in soil erosion, landslides, and flooding at lower levels.

In 1976, the Indian government put an end to commercial logging on slopes higher than 3,000 feet. By the mid-1980s, the people of Nepal were also replanting their forests.

Japanese Cedar
(*Cryptomeria japonica*)
Loved by the Japanese and protected there since the 1500s, these trees grow up to 150 feet tall. They have narrow, sharp, forward-pointing needles and round, spiny cones about .6 inches across.

Dawn Redwood
(*Metasequoia glyptostroboides*)
This tree, which likes a warm climate, grows up to about 115 feet. The leaves grow in two flat rows along the twigs and turn brick-red and fall in the autumn. The stalked cones are small and round.

Japanese Larch
(*Larix kaempferi*)
This 100-foot tall tree grows on Japanese mountains. The small cones have petal-shaped scales.

Chinese Fir
(*Cunninghamia lanceolata*)
One of China's most useful timber trees, the Chinese fir grows up to 150 feet tall. The needles are hard and pointed. The round cones, about 1.75 inches across, grow on the branch tips.

Deodar
(*Cedrus deodara*)
A very ornamental tree, this cedar is most important for its timber in India. Growing 180 to 250 feet tall, it has branches that droop at the ends. The smooth, upright, oblong cones are 4 inches long.

Indian Chir Pine
(*Pinus roxburghii*)
Most of India's turpentine comes from this 150-foot tall pine. The needles, which grow in bunches of three, are 12.5 inches long. The cones are 6 inches long and have long scales.

Himalayan conifers
Large conifer forests once covered the middle slopes of the Himalayas. If the trees are removed, the soil goes too, washed away by floods. Local folklore pays homage to the trees, but logging companies may not be so respectful until perhaps it is too late.

CONIFERS OF THE SOUTH

There are few coniferous forests in the southern hemisphere because there is less land and the climate is often unsuitable. However, conifers do grow in parts of South America, Africa, Australia, and New Zealand.

Before Europeans settled in New Zealand in the eighteenth century, the forests there had changed little for millions of years. They were very similar to the ancient forests in which the dinosaurs lived. Earlier settlers, the Maoris, cut trees for boatbuilding and cleared forests on a slash-and-burn system for farming. The Europeans quickly cleared much larger areas and introduced grazing animals such as sheep, cattle, deer, and rabbits, which fed on the tree seedlings, destroying them.

The Norfolk Island pine

On tiny Norfolk Island in the middle of the Pacific Ocean, halfway between Australia and the northernmost tip of New Zealand, grows a tree that is found naturally nowhere else in the world. It is the Norfolk Island pine (*Araucaria heterophylla*). Not really a pine, this tree is related to the monkey puzzle tree of South America. It is a tall tree, growing up to 200 feet in warm climates. Although from such a remote home, because of its beautiful shape it is familiar as a house-plant in greenhouses and conservatories in cooler countries. The branches grow in whorls around the trunk and smaller branchlets are arranged along the main branches similar to a fern frond. Young trees have soft needles, but they become harder as the tree grows older.

Kauri forests of New Zealand

Much of the remaining native forest is protected, and great efforts are being made to recreate areas of woodland close to the original.

18

Kauri
(*Agathis australis*)

Almost 99 percent of the magnificent kauri forests of New Zealand were felled in the nineteenth century. Now, these tall trees (150 feet) are protected. Their leaves are oval and leathery.

Monkey Puzzle tree
(*Araucaria araucana*)

A curiosity the world over, but a common sight on the slopes of its native Andes in South America, this 100-foot tall tree has broad, stiffly pointed leaves. The huge cones are 6.25 inches across.

Totara
(*Podocarpus totara*)

A slow-growing but hardy tree found only in New Zealand, the totara lives 1,000 years and can reach 120 feet. It was the most important source of timber for the Maoris. Each nutlike seed sits on a shallow, red, fleshy cup.

Oteniqua Yellow-wood
(*Podocarpus falcatus*)

One of the best timber trees of South Africa, it is restricted to small, protected forests. The leaves are long and narrow, and a green, berrylike scale covers the seed.

Alerce
(*Fitzroya cupressoides*)

This 150-foot tall, long-lived tree is important for timber in southern Chile. It grows on marshy ground and hillsides. The tiny round cones are only .3 inches across.

Rimu
(*Dacrydium cupressinum*)

Widespread throughout New Zealand, this 75-foot tall tree has graceful, "weeping" branches. The leaves are small, overlapping scales and the seed sits in a cup like an acorn.

TRUNKS AND ROOTS

Conifer seedlings may have two or many **cotyledons**, or seed-leaves, which open above the ground, and may last a year or longer. The seedling soon grows into a young tree. Conifers have a more regular pattern of branching than broad-leaved trees, and this means that young trees in particular can be very **symmetrical** or evenly shaped.

As the tree grows older, the arrangement of branches, twigs, and leaves gives each sort of tree its characteristic shape. The branching part of the tree is called its crown. Some conifers, for example spruces, firs, and Douglas firs, keep their familiar "fir-tree" shape even when old. Others such as pines, yew, and the cedar of Lebanon develop broader-shaped crowns, while cypresses are flame-or cone-shaped.

A tree needs strong, branched, woody roots to anchor it firmly in the ground. Each branchlet ends in very fine rootlets that absorb water and minerals such as nitrates and phosphates from the soil.

Stone Age conifers
Many conifers reach a great age. It is strange to think that when the ancient bristlecone pines of the White Mountains, California (pictured here) were seedlings, Stone Age Neolithic people were living in Europe. Gnarled and weather-beaten, these trees span the centuries from the Stone Age to the computer age.

The Tree Trunk

The outermost layer of a tree is the **bark**, a corky layer that protects it. Some species have very distinctive bark, which can help to identify the tree.

Just below the bark is a thin, living layer called **phloem**. The phloem is made up of fine tubes that carry sugars made in the leaves throughout the tree (see p. 22).

Beneath the phloem is a very thin layer called the **cambium**. The cambium contains a layer of living cells that grow and make the tree trunk a little thicker every year. When a tree is felled, each year's growth can be seen on the stump. The age of the tree can be found by counting these annual growth rings. We can also find out something about the climate during the long life of the tree. In dry years, the annual rings are narrower than in wet years.

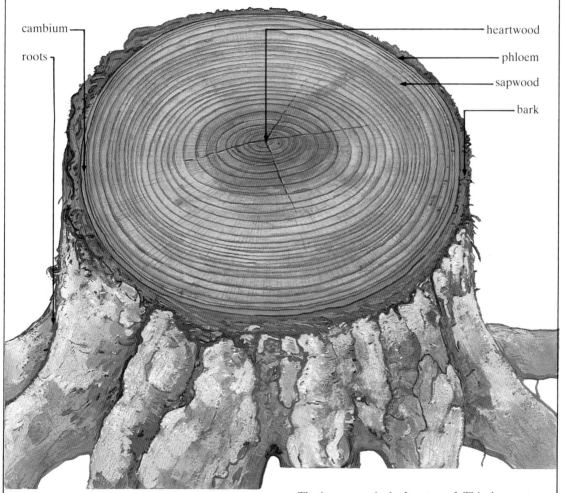

cambium

roots

heartwood

phloem

sapwood

bark

The rest of the trunk is the hard, useful material that we know as wood. The outer layer is called the **sapwood**. It is pale in color and is made up of **xylem** tubes that carry **sap** (water and minerals) from the roots to the leaves and buds.

The inner core is the **heartwood**. This does not conduct sap, but gives strength and support to the tree. In most trees, the heartwood is easy to see when the tree is felled, because it is darker in color than the sapwood. The color is due to the resin (see p. 42) stored in the heartwood.

LEAVES

Leaves make the food for the tree by a process called **photosynthesis**. In the leaf, the green pigment **chlorophyll** uses energy from sunlight to combine carbon dioxide gas from the air with water carried up by the roots from the soil to make sugar. The gas oxygen is also produced during this process. The gases carbon dioxide and oxygen enter and leave the leaf through tiny holes in its surface called **stomata**.

For photosynthesis to take place, the sun's rays have to shine upon the leaf. In a thick forest, sunlight does not reach the needles on the lower branches, so they die. This is why a forest conifer has a tall, straight trunk, with all the leafy branches at the top. A fir or spruce tree growing alone in an open space has leafy boughs sweeping the ground.

Most conifers keep their needles all year round and are often described as evergreen. Pine needles may only last two years; spruces and firs have needles that may last six to nine years. However, old conifer leaves are only shed a few at a time so the tree is never bare. Larches, dawn redwoods, and swamp cypresses behave like broad-leaved trees and shed all their leaves in autumn.

Weatherproof needles
Water is often scarce in regions where conifers grow. The summers may be hot and dry and the ground may freeze in winter, so although snow may lie thickly, it cannot be taken up by the tree. Needles have a hard, waxy skin that helps to prevent water being lost by evaporation from them. It also helps to protect the needles from frost damage in winter. The needles are very wind resistant, too. Even strong gales can blow through without damaging them. This allows conifers to grow taller and better than broad-leaved trees in windy places.

Pine Needles

Different groups of conifers have similar needles, but no two species are identical.

Pines have needles in bunches of two (Scotch pine), three (ponderosa pine, *P. ponderosa*), or five (sugar pine, *P. lambertiana*). They may be long – the long-leaf pine (*P. palustris*) has needles 18 inches long.

Spruce needles are short, usually stiff, and spiky. They grow in a spiral around the twig. When they fall, each needle leaves a little rough peg.

Fir needles are short and are not attached to the twigs on little pegs. They may be flat and leathery or sharp and spiky.

Larches, the true cedars (*Cedrus* species), and Japanese umbrella pine (*Sciadopitys verticillata*) have needles that grow in circles or whorls.

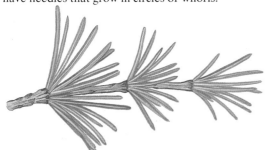

Some trees have flat, strap-shaped needles in two rows, for example the yew, the swamp cypress (*Taxodium distichum*), and the coast redwood.

The kauri and the yellow-woods have leathery leaves, sometimes broad (kauri) or narrow (oteniqua, *Podocarpus falcatus*).

Some leaves are small and scalelike, and grow close to the stems. They may be smooth (Lawson cypress, *Chamaecyparis lawsoniana*) or quite spiky (giant sequoia, *Sequoiadendron giganteum*).

MAKING SEEDS

Conifers do not have flowers, instead they have male and female cones. The female cone produces the egg or ovule and the male cone produces the male sex cell protected in a pollen grain. Once the pollen has been shed, the male cone falls from the tree. The pollen from the male cone is blown by the wind and lands on the female cone.

Growth of the cone
Some cones only take one year from pollination to the shedding of ripe seed. These are usually the smaller cones with thinner scales, such as larches and hemlocks. The very hard, woody pine cones take longer to develop. Scotch pine cones take up to three years to release their seeds.

This is called **pollination**. When the male sex cell **fertilizes** the ovule by joining or fusing with it, a seed is formed. The conifer seed develops on the surface of a female cone scale. It is not enclosed in a fruit, and so it is called a naked seed. Most species have male and female cones on each tree, but a few, including junipers, carry only male or female cones.

Young female cones are mostly yellowish-green, but some are brightly colored, for instance some pines, spruces, and larches have deep-pink cones. As they enlarge, they turn green, although there are some surprises. The cones of some fir trees, for example Delavay's silver fir (*Abies delavayi*), turn cobalt blue!

The male cone

Male cones are small and are borne near the ends of the branches. They consist of a central spike with tiny, overlapping scales. On the lower surface of each scale are the pollen sacs. The male cones usually grow and ripen in spring. When the pollen is ripe, the tiny scales open and the pollen sacs split to release the pollen. Conifer pollen is light and dusty and easily blown by the wind. Pine pollen grains even have minute air bladders to help them float through the air. Clouds of pollen fall from each tree. Most of it is wasted, and only a tiny amount finds its way to a young female cone.

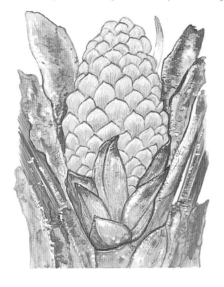

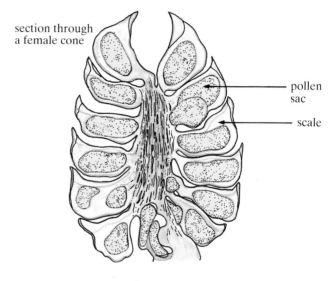

section through a female cone

pollen sac

scale

The female cone

These are also made up of closely overlapping scales attached to a central stalk. There may be only a few scales, or many, according to the species. The ovule develops on the upper surface of each scale. When they first appear in spring, the soft scales open to allow pollen to enter. The pollen grains stick to tiny droplets of water at the mouth of the ovule. Then the scales close. Pollination and the development of the seed takes place in the safety of the closed female cone.

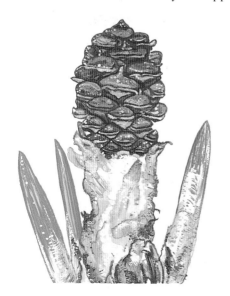

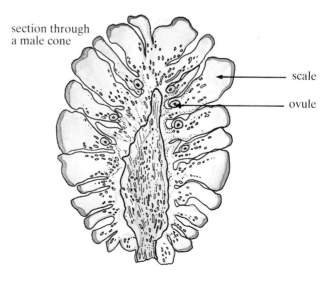

section through a male cone

scale

ovule

SEED DISPERSAL

By the time the seeds are ready to fall, the cones are brown and woody. In spring or early summer the warm sun dries out the cone, and the scales open. The light seeds, each with a papery wing, are spread by the wind. Even a gentle breeze is enough to carry the winged seed some distance from the parent tree.

Some of the largest and woodiest pine cones need much more than spring sunshine before they will open. Stone pines need the hot summer sun of the Mediterranean, and Californian pines need the heat of a very hot sun, or even a forest fire, before their cones will open. Knobcone pines (*Pinus attenuata*) have knobbly cones that only open after fire and they may remain on the tree 30 to 40 years before they are able to shed their seeds.

Seed dispersal by birds
The seeds of yellow-woods and yews are, like those of juniper, dispersed by birds. Blackbirds and thrushes are especially fond of the sweet, sticky aril of yew. The seeds of yew are very poisonous to animals and humans. Birds swallow them, but come to no harm. Their stomach juices do not digest the seeds, and they are passed out in the bird's droppings. The seeds are still able to grow or germinate.

Conifers without cones
Yellow-wood trees (*Podocarpus* species), plum yews (*Cephalotaxus* species), and true yews (*Taxus* species) do not have cones. Instead, the yellow-woods have a single scale on a short stalk. This scale grows larger and wraps around the ripening seed. The scale is often leathery and resinous. Plum yews are similar.

True yews are different: a single seed develops at the tip of a very tiny shoot in the **axil** of a leaf. As it ripens, the stem immediately below it swells around the seed to make a bright red, soft, fleshy cup called an **aril**.

26

Cone Facts

■ Fir and cedar cones grow upright on the branches. They are very resinous (they contain a lot of resin).

■ Spruce and pine cones hang downward. Cones of five-needled pines are very resinous. Douglas fir cones hang down, too.

■ Larch and Chinese fir have cone scales that open out and almost look like petals.

■ The tiniest cones are found on alerce (*Fitzroya cupressoides*) and some cypresses (*Chamaecyparis* species). They are between .3 and .5 inches across.

■ The smallest pine cones are those of the mountain pine (*Pinus mugo*), which are 1 to 2 inches long.

■ The longest pine cone is that of the sugar pine (*Pinus lambertiana*) – 2 feet long.

■ The heaviest pine cone belongs to the bigcone pine (*P. coulteri*). Before opening, these can weigh as much as 5 pounds. They also have large, sharp spines, one on each scale.

■ Pine cones are smooth and knobbly (the stone pine), bristly (the bristlecone pine; *P. aristata*), or very spiny (the prickly pine; *P. pungens*).

■ Redwoods and cypresses (*Cupressus* species) have round cones with only a few scales.

CONIFERS OF THE COLD

Forests can only exist in regions where the climate is suitable. Trees need at least 7·5 inches of rain each year and they also need summer temperatures of at least 50°F. The taiga forests grow in the cooler parts of North America, northern Europe, and Asia. At the southern edge of its range, the climate is too dry and grassland replaces the forest. At the northern edge, it becomes too cold for the forest to grow. Even so, in Siberia, the taiga extends well inside the Arctic Circle.

Toward the equator, the climate becomes warmer. However, on mountains the temperature falls with increasing height. So there are large areas of coniferous forest growing on the slopes of the world's mountain ranges.

The treeline

The highest level on a mountainside where trees are able to grow is called the treeline. This is not at the same height on all mountains as it depends on latitude, that is, the distance away from the equator (latitude 0°).

Larches, spruces, and junipers can live in the harsh conditions at the treeline. The narrow, pointed shape of spruce and fir trees ensures that snow slides off easily without damaging the branches.

Leafless in winter, the Dahurian larch (*Larix dahurica*) grows at the Arctic treeline in Siberia. Where the wind is often violent, the trees appear flag-shaped, with branches growing only on one side.

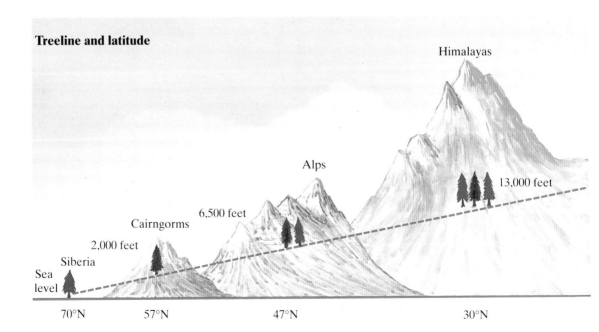

Treeline and latitude

Himalayas

Alps

13,000 feet

6,500 feet

Cairngorms

2,000 feet

Siberia

Sea level

70°N　　　57°N　　　　47°N　　　　　30°N

Plants of cold coniferous forests

When trees grow close together in a forest, their branches intermingle to form a **canopy**. The canopy of spruce and fir forests can be very dense, and can shade out 70 – 90 percent of the light, so that the forest floor is a dark and gloomy place.

The fallen conifer needles take a long time to rot and gradually build up into a thick layer beneath the trees. Unlike the fertile leaf-litter of a broad-leaved forest, the leaf-litter in a conifer forest is acid and infertile. This poor soil combined with the darkness of the forest means that few wild flowers or bushes can grow. Instead, mosses and lichens flourish.

Animals of the forest

Plant-eating animals of coniferous forests either depend on the conifers for food or on birches and grasses growing in clearings. The arolla pine (*Pinus cembra*) of European mountain slopes and the Siberian pine (*P. sibirica*) provide food for the nutcracker. This bird has a strong beak and can prize open the cone scales to get at the seeds. It also hides stores of seeds to eat another day. Some of these seeds are forgotten, and these grow into new trees, replenishing the forest.

Squirrels and many birds such as siskins, finches, and crossbills eat spruce, pine, and larch seeds. Other birds feed on the beetles, moths, and aphids that infest the trees. At ground level, the wood lemming feeds on the mosses of the taiga from Scandinavia to Siberia. Deer roam freely through the forests and are preyed on by wolves. Pine martens prey on the smaller animals and the eggs and nestlings of birds.

nutcracker

pine marten

crossbill

siskin

red squirrel

MILD, MOIST FORESTS

In the coastal forests of western North America, there are no frosts or dry seasons, and the forest floor is a thick carpet of ferns, mosses, and lichens. Grasses grow in clearings. Not surprisingly, many of the animals of this forest are good climbers. Wherever there are cones, there are squirrels like the Douglas squirrel of these forests, to eat the seeds. The North American porcupine eats the tender young shoots of spruce and pine. Although slow, its strong claws help it to climb up to 65 feet. Another agile climber is the American marten, which preys on birds and squirrels.

The kauri and yellow-wood forests of the North Island, New Zealand, have a similar climate to the western coastal forests of North America. Instead of redwoods, spruces, and Douglas fir, there are kauri, totara, rimu, and kahikatea. On the forest floor, a tangle of ferns and mosses grows. Tree ferns are characteristic of these forests. The black tree fern (*Cyathea medullaris*) has a crown of fronds 35 feet across on a trunk up to 60 feet tall.

North American forests
Large areas of these forests are now reserves or national parks. The Olympia National Park in Washington is one of these. These parks ensure the survival of the trees and are refuges for animals that, like the North American black bear, were once widespread. These bears are good climbers and will eat almost anything that comes their way – seeds, berries, eggs, insects, or small animals. Wapiti and black-tailed deer browse on vegetation in the clearings.

Woodpeckers of Coniferous Forests

Insect-eating woodpeckers often depend on mature trees for food and nesting sites. When forests are felled, they are among the first to suffer.

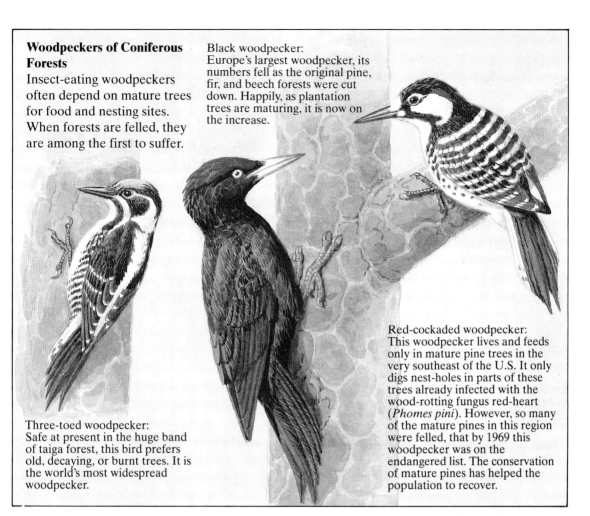

Black woodpecker:
Europe's largest woodpecker, its numbers fell as the original pine, fir, and beech forests were cut down. Happily, as plantation trees are maturing, it is now on the increase.

Red-cockaded woodpecker:
This woodpecker lives and feeds only in mature pine trees in the very southeast of the U.S. It only digs nest-holes in parts of these trees already infected with the wood-rotting fungus red-heart (*Phomes pini*). However, so many of the mature pines in this region were felled, that by 1969 this woodpecker was on the endangered list. The conservation of mature pines has helped the population to recover.

Three-toed woodpecker:
Safe at present in the huge band of taiga forest, this bird prefers old, decaying, or burnt trees. It is the world's most widespread woodpecker.

Moist forests of New Zealand

Originally there were no native mammals except bats in these forests, but insects and other invertebrates (animals without backbones) were abundant. However, rats, cats, wild pigs, opossums, deer, and stoats have all been introduced and much of the original forest has gone. Many of the native birds that lived there are also disappearing. Fortunately, the most famous New Zealand bird, the flightless common kiwi, is not endangered. It lives in the dense forest, feeding on insects and grubs on the forest floor.

HUMAN-MADE FORESTS

M uch of temperate Europe was once almost covered with forests. Only the mountain tops and wetlands were treeless. These native woodlands were mostly broad-leaved trees, for example oak, ash, beech, sycamore, and sweet chestnut. Tribes settling in Europe started to clear the forests to build homes and farm the land. As time went by, the population increased and more and more land was cleared. Timber was needed to build ships, to fight wars, and to fuel the Industrial Revolution. Farmland was needed for crops and domestic animals. By the early 1900s most of the natural forest had been lost.

Many of the trees that were planted to take the place of the lost forests were conifers. They are fast-growing and easy to manage, and can be used for many purposes. These commercially managed forests provide much of the wood used in the timber industry (see p. 38).

Plantations

Trees that are planted for commercial purposes are planted in straight rows, just like any other crop. Areas where trees have been planted in this way are called **plantations**. But the oaks and beeches that were felled so long ago are not the trees being replanted. These trees, although producing excellent timber, grow very slowly. Instead, fast-growing, often foreign, conifers are planted. Many come from North America and grow quickly in temperate climates (see p. 14). The sitka spruce, Corsican pine, Norway spruce, and lodgepole pine are planted most often in these woods.

Wildlife in the plantations

Plantations are artificial woodlands. The rows of trees are planted in blocks, so that each block contains trees all the same age. Blocks are separated by wide, grassy areas called rides for the forester's vehicles, and to act as firebreaks.

Trees are planted when they are three years old. For about the first ten years, grasses, wild flowers, and bushes grow among the trees. As the trees grow taller, they form a canopy and the ground is too dark for grasses and flowers to grow. Except for thinning out trees, a block will be clear-felled when the trees are about 70 years old.

Red and roe deer also thrive in the plantations. With no natural predators, their numbers have to be controlled. Deer can do a lot of damage, especially to young trees.

Clearings

The rides of plantations provide a different kind of habitat, a clearing between blocks of trees. Wild flowers and bushes grow there, attracting insects and birds, rats, mice, and hedgehogs. Birds of prey hunt along the rides. There are no old, hollow trees, so to encourage bats and birds, people have put up boxes.

THE LIVING FOREST

A forest is not simply a place where a large number of trees grow, it is made up of groups or communities of plants and animals. Each community occupies a different part of the forest – the forest floor, a clearing, or the forest canopy. The relationship between these communities, together with the trees, form the forest ecosystem. So any threat to the forest is a threat to the whole ecosystem.

Foresters remove selected trees, or small groups of trees, by selective felling. It need not damage the forest as a whole. Trees naturally age and fall, creating temporary clearings. The extra light and space gives seedlings and young trees a chance to grow. However, selective felling can remove too many of the best trees and, once these have been taken, they cannot contribute their seeds to the forest. Many conifers take hundreds of years to reach their prime, so it also takes hundreds of years to replace those that have been chopped down.

Fire

In warmer parts of the world, for example the coast redwood forest, fires break out spontaneously (without being lit) and are a natural part of the forest environment. However, coast redwoods and giant sequoias have thick, insulating bark that does not burn easily. The leaf litter is burned, so that it does not build up into a thick layer, and the nutrients are released back into the soil. Some pines depend on the heat of fires to open their cones. Enough seeds survive to germinate and grow after a fire.

However, in the cooler taiga forests, fires can do great damage. The trees do not have thick bark, and as the resinous conifers burn quickly, it is often very difficult to control these fires. In 1915, a huge forest fire in Siberia burned an area one-third the size of Europe.

Clear felling

Clear felling is when all the trees are cut down, and the branches, stumps, and roots burned. Clearing a forest in this way severely disrupts the animal and plant life. If all the forest in a region is felled, the plants and animals that are special to the forest may be lost.

Cutting down a forest also affects the surrounding environment. When heavy rain falls on the forest canopy, the dense layer of needles slows it down. Instead of beating down onto the ground, it trickles and drips. When the rain soaks into the soil, the tree roots also slow down the speed of the water. These effects are especially important on a hillside. The bare soil exposed after the trees have been felled is readily washed away, leaving bare rocks, which make it difficult for trees to regenerate (grow again).

The Sierra Nevada

Fires were a natural occurrence on the slopes of the Sierra Nevada where giant sequoias grow. However, the remaining groves of these splendid trees are now a tourist attraction, and these fires are prevented. The thick layer of leaf litter and the trampling of the tourists' feet prevents the growth of new seedlings, so the forest cannot regenerate naturally. Young trees are raised in nurseries and planted back into the wild.

ACID RAIN

When fossil fuels like oil and coal are burned, many kinds of gases are released into the atmosphere, for example, carbon dioxide, sulfur dioxide, nitrogen oxides, and water. Sulfur dioxide and nitrogen oxides are soluble and they will dissolve in rain as it falls to make dilute acids. The more of these gases there are in the air, the more acidic the rain will be. The rain falls as dilute sulfuric and nitric acids. If acid rain lands on chalky soils, it is neutralized or inactivated and does little damage. When it rains down on soils poor in chalk or lime, it increases the acidity of the soil, rivers, and lakes. Acid rain slowly destroys many plants and trees and this is especially noticeable in coniferous forests.

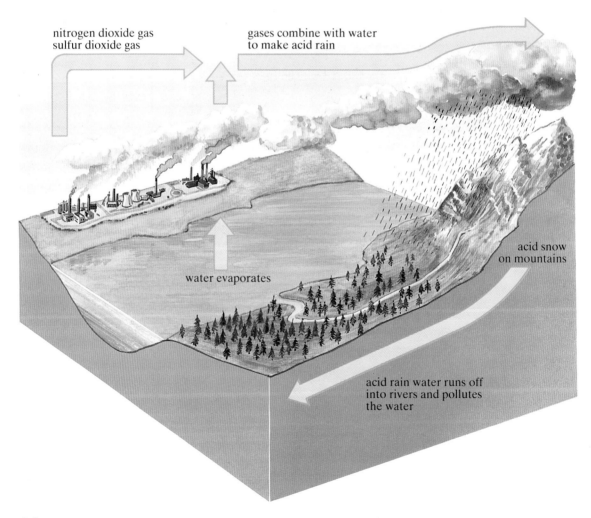

nitrogen dioxide gas
sulfur dioxide gas

gases combine with water
to make acid rain

acid snow
on mountains

water evaporates

acid rain water runs off
into rivers and pollutes
the water

Acid Rain – Finding a Solution

The problem is not a simple one. Conifers are certainly being damaged, but exactly how acid rain harms them is less well understood. Solutions to this problem are not straightforward.

■ About 60 percent of all sulfur dioxide in the atmosphere is released naturally from volcanoes and marine organisms.

■ Sulfur can be removed from coal before it is burned, but for each ton of sulfur removed, up to 10 tons of coal are wasted.

■ Sulfur dioxide can be removed from smoke before it reaches the atmosphere. To do this it is passed through water containing powdered limestone. But a power station burning 4 million tons of coal every year would need about 500,000 tons of limestone every year. Where would this come from? Limestone is quarried from the ground. The enormous amount needed in the U.K. alone would create even more problems.

■ Removing the sulfur or sulfur dioxide would increase the cost of electricity.

■ Higher costs of coal-generated electricity might result in more nuclear power stations. There would be no acid rain from these, but the even greater problem of nuclear waste.

Acid rain from afar

Acid rain from industrial smokestacks does not necessarily affect the country of origin. Scandinavia suffers the effects of acid rain from Britain, Europe, and the western U.S.S.R., and Canada's acid rain comes from the U.S.

The Black Forest

The Black Forest in southern Germany is a region of rolling hills clothed in fir and beech woods. It is rich in animal life: red and roe deer, red squirrels, wild boar, and birds and is an area of outstanding natural beauty. However, many trees have been affected by acid rain and are sick or already dead, and the natural wildlife is also suffering. New England and Canadian forests also have dead and dying trees.

THE TIMBER INDUSTRY

Wood is still one of the world's most important resources. It is hard-wearing, tough, and yet pleasant to use and look at. Materials such as plastics, fiberglass, and light metals have replaced wood for some purposes, but wood will always be in demand.

Each species of tree has its own special grain, which can be seen as a pattern in the wood. It is made by the growth of cells in the tree trunk. Some conifers yield fine, long-lasting timber as their heartwood is full of resins that act as a natural protection. Douglas fir, western red cedar, white pine, and cedar of Lebanon are timbers that can be used for indoor and outdoor building and carpentry.

Wood from pines and larches is used for furniture, builder's planks, fences, and joinery. Chemicals called wood preservatives can be put onto these woods to protect them from attack by insects and molds. Some of the fastest-growing conifers are spruces and firs, which are used for building purposes, and to make wood pulp for paper.

Once at the sawmill, the logs are cut up in a number of ways.
■ They may be debarked and used as poles.
■ They may be sawn into planks.
■ They may be "pared" into thin sheets to be used as a wood veneer on sheets of pressed wood or plywood.
■ Poor-quality wood and timber yard scraps are chipped and made into pressed wood, or pulped for paper.

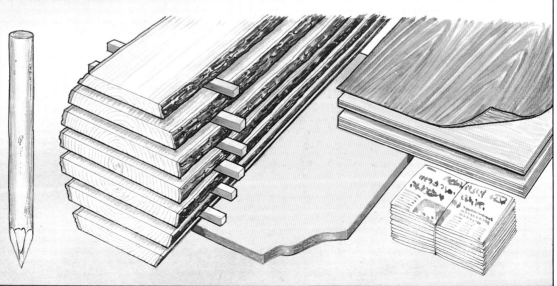

Plantations and the environment

In many countries, people want to plant conifer trees on unspoiled areas of upland or heathland. This can lead to disputes between the forestry companies and conservationists. For example, in northern Scotland, in the U.K., the Flow Country is under threat. The Flow Country is an almost flat area of a very wet peatland known as blanket bog. It is a relatively unique area – a large, remote wilderness with a wet, windy climate. A rich mixture of rare mosses and bog plants grows there and many birds, for example, dunlin, golden plover, black-throated diver, greenshank, short-eared owl, and merlin, breed there.

Unlike most of the U.K., the Flow Country is not natural woodland as it is far too wet and windy. So it is most unlikely that trees will grow well. However, the Forestry Commission and private companies together aim to plant up to 15 percent (250,000 acres) with North American conifers. About 150,000 acres have been planted already. The effect is not yet known, but there are fears that the bog will dry out and this unique area will be lost.

Why conifers?

Young conifers can be planted close together in a plantation, and since the wood is fairly light, they can be felled and transported easily. Conifers grow quickly, so companies and governments are willing to invest money in conifer planting because they will make a quick profit on their investment. In the U.S. more trees are now planted annually than are felled.

PAPER-MAKING

At the beginning of the twentieth century, there were no paper tissues or towels, paper bags were not in general use, and school children wrote on slates. Now we take paper for granted. Many relatively new paper products, especially disposable ones, are considered to be daily essentials. In the richer countries, each person uses about 265 pounds of paper a year. In the poorer, undeveloped countries, each person uses about 18 pounds of paper a year.

Paper Production

To make various types and qualities of paper, the pulp is treated in different ways. Paper for drawing or writing needs a smooth, water-resistant surface so that inks do not spread out and run. China clay and size (glue) are added for this. Pure white paper is made by bleaching the pulp. Sometimes, colors are added to the bleached pulp. Unbleached paper is brownish or straw-colored.

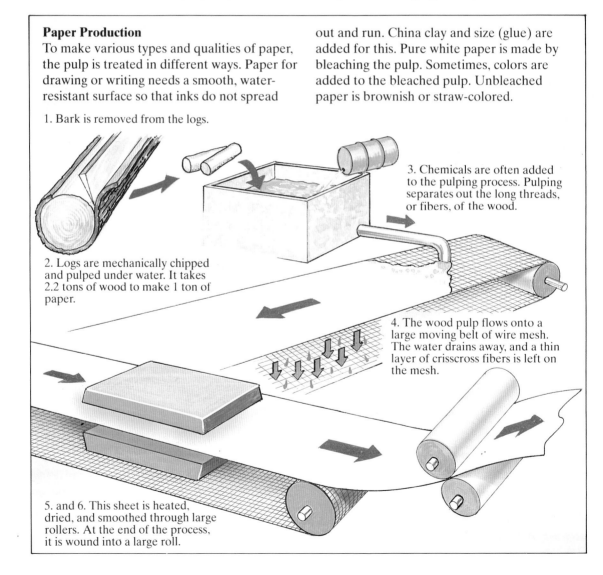

1. Bark is removed from the logs.

2. Logs are mechanically chipped and pulped under water. It takes 2.2 tons of wood to make 1 ton of paper.

3. Chemicals are often added to the pulping process. Pulping separates out the long threads, or fibers, of the wood.

4. The wood pulp flows onto a large moving belt of wire mesh. The water drains away, and a thin layer of crisscross fibers is left on the mesh.

5. and 6. This sheet is heated, dried, and smoothed through large rollers. At the end of the process, it is wound into a large roll.

Paper-making and pollution

It takes a lot of water to pulp logs, so pulp mills are usually built beside large rivers. Unfortunately, the waste from making wood pulp can cause pollution when it is dumped back into the river. The process used to bleach the pulp is usually based on chlorine-containing chemicals, poisonous substances often used in disinfectants and pesticides. However, an even more poisonous chemical, dioxin, is made during this bleaching process. Dioxin enters the river or ocean in the waste water from the pulp mill. Baltic Sea fishers say that dioxin from Swedish pulp mills is killing the fish and threatening their livelihood.

Waste paper

The amount of waste paper from the U.S. alone in one year is equivalent to 4 1/4 million trucks full. Of course, no one in developed countries would like to be without items such as newspapers, books, or toilet paper.

However it is possible to reuse some kinds of waste paper, which can be shredded and pulped in much the same way as logs. Recycled paper actually uses less energy to produce. Egg cartons, stationery, newspapers, and packing are all items on a growing list that are made partially or completely from recycled paper. One of the biggest problems is collecting the waste paper.

USES PAST AND PRESENT

As well as their uses for buildings, furniture-making, and paper production, conifers give us many other useful products. Pine kernels from about 18 kinds of pines are eaten in many parts of the northern hemisphere. They are nutritious (a good quality food), although some taste rather strongly of turpentine. Perhaps the most popular are the kernels of the stone pine. This pine grows on hillsides around the Mediterranean. The kernels are an ingredient in the cooking of many of these countries, especially Lebanon. They are very good to eat and are sold throughout Europe. The large seeds of the monkey puzzle tree are roasted and eaten in South America. The juicy "berries" of the common juniper are a traditional flavoring for meat and game dishes in many countries.

Resin

Most conifers contain resin. It is an aromatic, sticky liquid. It oozes from the trunk or branches when they are cut or damaged. When the resin dries it forms a protective layer. It gives some species a characteristic smell, for example, grand fir needles have a strong scent of tangerine and nootka cypress has a disagreeable, oily smell.

Some conifers, pines in particular, contain so much resin that it can be collected, or tapped, from the tree trunk. Part of the bark is deliberately cut and the resin drains into a container. Resin can be separated into liquid (turpentine), and a solid (rosin). Turpentine is still used in some paints and rosin is used in glues and varnishes.

Flavorings

Gin is a spirit distilled from rye grains and flavored with juniper "berries." Most gin is produced in the Netherlands. The berries are collected from wild plants. Common juniper grows in North America, Europe, and central Asia. The strongest-flavored berries come from the warmest countries.

Retsina is a Greek wine flavored with resin from the aleppo pine. Though popular in Greece, its strongly resinous flavor is an acquired taste for other people.

Longbows and medicines

In Europe, yew wood was once of great value for making longbows. As the leaves and seeds are very poisonous, it was often planted in walled churchyards, out of reach of grazing animals. Western tribes of Native Americans also used yew for their bows as well as spear handles and fish hooks.

As well as flavorings for food and drink, oils made from junipers have a long history of medicinal uses, including the treatment of skin disorders. However, some like those from the rock cedar (*Juniperus sabina*; pictured below), which contain a poisonous chemical called sabinol, are rarely used these days as they are considered to be too dangerous.

43

GLOSSARY

ARIL – The bright, fleshy covering around seeds from trees such as yews.

AXIL – The point where a leaf or branch meets a stem.

BARK – The outer layer of tree trunk and branches. It is often rough and quite thick.

CAMBIUM – The growing layer that makes the tree trunk a little thicker each year.

CANOPY – The top layer of leaves, which in woods is made up of the crowns of trees.

CHLOROPHYLL – The green pigment of plants that absorbs energy from light to make food by photosynthesis.

CONE – The reproductive unit of many gymnosperms. Male cones produce pollen, and female cones protect the developing seeds.

COTYLEDONS – The first simple leaves that appear from a seed when it germinates.

CROWN – The upper part of a tree, made up of its branches, twigs, and leaves.

DECIDUOUS – Trees that lose their leaves at the end of each growing season.

ECOSYSTEM – Communities of animals and plants and the environments in which they live.

FERTILIZATION – The entry and joining of a male pollen cell with the female ovule.

GYMNOSPERMS – A group of flowerless plants that have seeds mostly contained in woody cones, or in fleshy scales.

HEARTWOOD – The nonliving, but very strong, wood that makes up the central core of the tree trunk.

OVULE – The female "cell" that grows into a seed after fertilization.

PHLOEM – The narrow layer beneath the bark that carries sugars from the leaves to other parts of the tree.

PHOTOSYNTHESIS – The process in green plants that uses the energy in sunlight to turn carbon dioxide gas and water into sugars, releasing oxygen.

PLANTATION – An area where trees are planted and grown by foresters for commercial reasons.

POLLEN GRAIN – A male "cell" that after pollination, fertilizes an ovule so that it can grow into a seed.

POLLINATION – This happens when the pollen from a male cone lands on the slightly open scales of a young female cone.

SAP – The watery juice in living plant cells.

SAPWOOD – The living layer of wood through which water taken up by the roots passes up the tree.

SEED – A fully developed, fertilized ovule. It contains an embryo and a food store, and can grow into a new plant.

STAND – An area of natural woodland where only a single kind of tree is found.

STOMATA – The tiny holes in the surface of a leaf through which gases and water vapor can pass.

SYMMETRICAL – The same shape all the way round.

XYLEM – Woody cells that conduct water in the sapwood.

CONIFERS IN THIS BOOK

Aleppo pine (*Pinus halepensis*)
Alerce (*Fitzroya cupressoides*)
Arolla pine (*Pinus cembra*)
Atlas cedar (*Cedrus atlantica*)
Bigcone pine (*Pinus coulteri*)
Bristlecone pine (*Pinus aristata*)
Cedar of Lebanon (*Cedrus libani*)
Chinese fir (*Cunninghamia lanceolata*)
Coast redwood (*Sequoia sempervirens*)
Common juniper (*Juniperus communis*)
Corsican pine (*Pinus nigra* var. *maritima*)
Dahurian larch (*Larix dahurica*)
Dawn redwood (*Metasequoia glyptostroboides*)
Delavay's silver fir (*Abies delavayi*)
Deodar (*Cedrus deodara*)
Douglas fir (*Pseudotsuga menziesii*)
European larch (*Larix decidua*)
European silver fir (*Abies alba*)
Giant or grand fir (*Abies grandis*)
Indian chir pine (*Pinus roxburghii*)
Japanese cedar (*Cryptomeria japonica*)
Japanese larch (*Larix kaempferi*)
Japanese umbrella pine (*Sciadopitys verticillata*)
Kahikatea (*Podocarpus dacrydiodes*)
Kauri (*Agathis australis*)
Knobcone pine (*Pinus attenuata*)
Lawson cypress (*Chamaecyparis lawsoniana*)
Lodgepole pine (*Pinus contorta*)
Long-leaf pine (*Pinus palustris*)
Maritime pine (*Pinus pinaster*)
Monkey puzzle (*Araucaria araucana*)
Monterey cypress (*Cupressus macrocarpa*)
Mountain pine (*Pinus mugo*)
Noble fir (*Abies nobilis*)
Nootka cypress (*Chamaecyparis nootkatensis*)
Norfolk Island pine (*Araucaria heterophylla*)
Norway spruce (*Picea abies*)
Oteniqua yellow-wood (*Podocarpus falcatus*)
Plum yews (*Cephalotaxus* species)
Ponderosa pine (*Pinus ponderosa*)
Prickly pine (*Pinus pungens*)
Rimu (*Dacrydium cupressinum*)
Rock cedar (*Juniperus sabina*)
Scotch pine (*Pinus sylvestris*)

Siberian pine (*Pinus sibirica*)
Sitka spruce (*Picea sitchensis*)
Stone pine (*Pinus pinea*)
Sugar pine (*Pinus lambertiana*)
Swamp cypress (*Taxodium distichum*)
Totara (*Podocarpus totara*)
Wellingtonia (*Sequoiadendron giganteum*)
Western hemlock (*Tsuga heterophylla*)
Western red cedar (*Thuja plicata*)
Yew (*Taxus baccata*)

FURTHER READING

For children:
Tree by David Burnie; Knopf, 1988.
The Blossom on the Bough: A Book of Trees by Anne O. Dowden; Harper, 1975.
Trees Alive by Sarah R. Riedman; Lothrop, 1974.

For adults:
Field Guide to Eastern Trees by G.A. Petrides; Houghton Mifflin, 1988.
The Gardener's Illustrated Encyclopedia of Trees & Shrubs by Brian Davis; Rodale Press, 1987.
Ornamental Conifers by Julie Grace; Timber Press, 1983.
Trees by Keith Rushforth; Exeter Books, 1983.

INDEX

A
Abies alba 12
Abies delavayi 24
Abies grandis 11
Abies nobilis 8
acid rain 36-37
Africa 12, 13, 14, 18, 19
Agathis australis 19
aleppo pine 13, 43
alerce 19, 27
algae 6
animals 29, 30, 31, 33, 35, 37
Araucaria araucana 6, 9, 19
Araucaria heterophylla 18
aril 26
arolla pine 29
Asia 9, 28, 43
Atlas cedar 12
Atlas mountains 12
Australia 14, 18

B
bark 21, 34
bigcone pine 27
birds 29, 31, 33, 37, 39
Black Forest 37
black tree fern 30
bristlecone pine 20, 27

C
Californian pine 26
cambium 21
Canada 10, 11, 28, 34, 37
cedar 23, 27
cedar of Lebanon 12, 20, 38
Cedrus atlantica 12
Cedrus deodara 17
Cedrus libani 12
Cedrus species 23
Cephalotaxaceae 6, 26
Chamaecyparis species 27
Chamaecyparis lawsoniana 23

Chamaecyparis nootkatensis 11
China 16, 17
Chinese fir 17, 27
chlorophyll 22
clear felling 33, 35
coast redwood 8, 15, 23, 34
cones 8, 24-25, 26-27, 29, 30, 34
Corsican pine 12, 13, 32
cotyledons 20
crown 8, 9, 20
Cryptomeria japonica 16
Cunninghamia lanceolata 17
Cupressaceae 6, 27
Cyathea medullaris 30
cycads 6
cypresses 6, 14, 20, 27

D
Dacrydium cupressinum 19
dahurian larch 28
dawn redwood 16, 17, 22
Delavay's silver fir 24
deodar 17
Douglas fir 8, 15, 20, 27, 30, 38

E
ecosystem 34
Europe 10, 12, 13, 14, 18, 29, 32, 37, 42, 43
European larch 13
European silver fir 12
Everglades 14

F
ferns 6, 30
fertilization 24-25
fire 34, 35
firs 9, 14, 20, 22, 23, 24, 27, 28, 29, 38
Fitzroya cupressoides 19, 27, 38
Flow Country 39
flowering plants 6
fungi 6

G
General Sherman tree 8, 9
giant sequoia 9, 23, 34, 35
ginkgo 6
gnetatae 6
grand, or giant, fir 11, 42
grasses 29, 30, 33
gymnosperms 6, 8, 9

H
heartwood 21, 38
hemlocks 24
Himalayan conifers 17
Howard Libbey tree 8

I
India 16, 17
Indian chir pine 17
insects 29, 30, 31, 33

J
Japanese cedar 16
Japanese larch 16
Japanese umbrella pine 23
juniper 6, 12, 24, 26, 28, 42, 43
Juniperus communis 12
Juniperus sabina 43

K
kahikatea 30
kauri 18-19, 23, 30
knobcone pine 26

L
larches 9, 13, 22, 23, 24, 27, 28, 38
Larix dahurica 28
Larix decidua 13
Larix kaempferi 16
Lawson cypress 23
lichens 6, 29, 30
lodgepole pine 15, 32
long-leaf pine 23

M
maritime pine 13
Metasequoia glyptostroboides
16, 17, 22
monkey puzzle tree 6, 9, 18,
19, 42
mosses 6, 29, 30
mountain pine 27

N
needles 22-23
Nepal 16
New Zealand 9, 14, 18-19, 30,
31
noble fir 8
nootka cypress 11, 42
Norfolk Island pine 18
North America 11, 14, 28, 30,
32, 34, 35, 43
Norway spruce 13, 32

O
oteniqua yellow-wood 19, 23
ovule 8, 24-25

P
paper 40-41
phloem 21
photosynthesis 22
Picea abies 13
Picea sitchensis 9, 15, 32
Pinaceae 6, 9, 14, 20, 27
pine kernels 42
pines 6, 9, 14, 20, 27, 30, 38
Pinus aristata 27
Pinus attenuata 26
Pinus cembra 29
Pinus contorta 15, 32
Pinus coulteri 27
Pinus halepensis 13, 43
Pinus lambertiana 23
Pinus mugo 27
Pinus nigra 12
Pinus nigra var. *maritima* 13
Pinus palustris 23
Pinus pinaster 13
Pinus pinea 13, 26, 27, 42
Pinus ponderosa 23
Pinus pungens 27

Pinus roxburghii 17
Pinus sibirica 29
Pinus sylvestris 12, 23, 24
plantations 32-33, 39
plum yews 6, 26
Podocarpaceae 6, 9, 26
Podocarpus falcatus 19, 23
Podocarpus totara 19, 30
poisons 26, 43
pollen grain 8, 24-25
pollination 24-25
ponderosa pine 23
prickly pine 27
Pseudotsuga menziesii 8, 15,
20, 38

R
redwoods 6, 8, 9, 23, 27, 30
resin 21, 27, 38, 42, 43
rimu 19, 30
rock cedar 43

S
sapwood 21
scales 25, 26, 27
Sciadopitys verticillata 23
Scotch pine 12, 23, 24
seeds 8, 24-25, 26, 29
Sequoia sempervirens 8, 15,
23, 34
Sequoiadendron giganteum
9, 23, 34, 35
Siberia 10, 28, 29, 34
Siberian pine 29
Sierra Nevada 11, 35
sitka spruce 9, 15, 32
soil erosion 16, 35
South America 9, 18-19
Soviet Union 10, 37
spruce 9, 14, 20, 22, 23, 24, 27,
28, 29, 30, 38
stands 10
stomata 22
stone pine 13, 26, 27, 42
sugar pine 23, 27
swamp cypress 14, 22, 23

T
taiga 10, 28-29, 31, 34

Tasmania 9
Taxaceae 6, 26
Taxodiaceae 6
Taxodium distichum 23
Taxus baccata 12
Thuja plicata 15
Tibet 16
timber 38-39
totara 19, 30
treeline 28
trunk 8, 20-21
Tsuga heterophylla 15

U
United Kingdom 12, 13, 14
37, 39, 41
United States 11, 14, 20, 30,
34, 35, 37, 43

W
Western hemlock 15
Western red cedar 15, 38
woodpeckers 31

X
xylem 21

Y
yellow-woods 6, 9, 23, 26, 30
yews 6, 12, 20, 23, 26, 43